W9-BMR-340

To:

_____

From:

_____

Date:

_____

FAMILY
CHRISTIAN
PRESS

Promises & Prayers

for Moms

FCP
FAMILY
CHRISTIAN
PRESS

PROMISES & PRAYERS
for Moms

©2002 Family Christian Press

All rights reserved. Except for brief quotations used in reviews, articles or other media, no part of this book may be reproduced or transmitted in any form or by any means, electronic or mechanical, including photocopying, recording, or by information storage or retrieval system, without permission by the publisher.

FAMILY CHRISTIAN PRESS
Grand Rapids, MI 49530

ISBN 1-58334-131-5

The quoted ideas expressed in this book (but not scripture verses) are not, in all cases, exact quotations, as some have been edited for clarity and brevity. In all cases, the author has attempted to maintain the speaker's original intent. In some cases, quoted material for this book was obtained from secondary sources, primarily print media. While every effort was made to ensure the accuracy of these sources, the accuracy cannot be guaranteed. For additions, deletions, corrections or clarifications in future editions of this text, please write FAMILY CHRISTIAN PRESS.

Certain elements of this text, including quotations, stories, and selected groupings of Bible verses, have appeared, in part or in whole, in publications produced by Brighton Books of Nashville, TN; these excerpts are used with permission.

All scripture quotations, unless otherwise indicated, are taken from the HOLY BIBLE, NEW INTERNATIONAL VERSION ©. NIV ©. Copyright © 1973, 1978, 1984, by International Bible Society. Used by permission of Zondervan Publishing House. All rights reserved.

Scripture taken from *THE MESSAGE*. Copyright © 1993, 1994,1995,1996. Used by permission of NavPress Publishing Group.

Scripture taken from the NEW AMERICAN STANDARD BIBLE®, Copyright © 1960, 1962, 1963, 1968, 1971, 1972, 1973, 1975, 1977, 1995 by The Lockman Foundation. Used by permission.

Scripture quotations marked (NKJV) are taken from The Holy Bible, New King James Version, Copyright © 1982 by Thomas Nelson, Inc. Used by permission.

Scripture quotations marked (NLT) are taken from The Holy Bible, New Living Translation, Copyright © 1996. Used by permission of Tyndale House Publishers, Incorporated, Wheaton, Illinois 60189. All rights reserved.

Printed in the United States of America
Cover Design & Page Layout: *Bart Dawson*

2 3 4 5 6 7 8 9 10 • 03 04 05 06 07 08 09 10

For Moms Everywhere

Table of Contents

INTRODUCTION

*I*n your hands, you hold a book entitled *Promises and Prayers for Moms*. Perhaps you received this book as a gift from a loving child or husband. Or, perhaps, amid the hustle and bustle of your daily life, you picked up this little book of your own accord. Either way, you will be blessed *if* you take the promises on these pages to heart.

This text addresses 72 topics. Each brief chapter contains Bible verses, a quotation from a noted Christian thinker, and a prayer. The ideas in each chapter are powerful reminders of God's commandments and of the joy and abundance He promises His children.

Motherhood is both a priceless blessing from God *and* an incredibly demanding responsibility. If you answer to the name "Mom," "Mother," "Mommy," or some variation thereof, you already know the joys of being a mother…and the demands. This book is intended to remind you that God stands ready, willing, and able to help.

ABUNDANCE

...I am come that they might have life, and that they might have it more abundantly.

—John 10:10 KJV

Success, success to you, and success to those who help you, for your God is with you....

—I Chronicles 12:18 NIV

Have faith in the LORD your God and you will be upheld; have faith in his prophets and you will be successful.

—II Chronicles 20:20 NIV

Thou wilt show me the path of life: in thy presence is fulness of joy; at thy right hand there are pleasures for evermore.

—Psalm 16:11 KJV

Delight thyself also in the LORD; and he shall give thee the desires of thine heart.

—Psalm 37:4 KJV

*J*esus promises that we can have abundance through Him. But, every mother knows that some days are so busy and so hurried that abundance seems a distant promise. It is not. Every day, we can claim the spiritual abundance that God promises for our lives...and we should.

———◆———

Get ready for God to show you not only His pleasure, but His approval.

—*Joni Eareckson Tada*

—A PRAYER—

*T*hank You, Dear Lord, for the abundant life that is mine through Your Son Jesus. In all that I say and do, let me share Your message of abundance with my family, my friends, and my community. Give me courage, Lord, to claim the spiritual riches that you have promised, and help me to share Your abundance with all who cross my path.

—*Amen*

ACCEPTING CHRIST

For God so loved the world, that he gave his only begotten Son, that whosoever believeth in him should not perish, but have everlasting life.

—John 3:16 KJV

For the wages of sin is death, but the gift of God is eternal life in Christ Jesus our Lord.

—Romans 6:23 NIV

Jesus answered and said unto her, Whosoever drinketh of this water shall thirst again: but whosoever drinketh of the water that I shall give him shall never thirst; but the water that I shall give him shall be in him a well of water springing up into everlasting life.

—John 4:13-14 KJV

Verily, verily, I say unto you, He that believeth on me hath everlasting life.

—John 6:47 KJV

*G*od loves you and your family. God's love for you is so great that He sent His only Son to this earth to die for your sins and to offer you the priceless gift of eternal life.

———⧫———

Turn your life over to Christ today, and your life will never be the same.

—Billy Graham

—A PRAYER—

*D*ear Lord, you invited me to join Your family, and I said yes. I confessed that Jesus was my Lord and Savior, and You saved me. I choose, this day, to live in such a way that others, especially my children, might also accept Christ as their Savior. Let all who cross my path see my love for You reflected through my words and my deeds.

—Amen

ADVERSITY

We are troubled on every side, yet not distressed; we are perplexed, but not in despair; persecuted, but not forsaken; cast down, but not destroyed....

—II Corinthians 4:8-9 KJV

They do not fear bad news; they confidently trust the Lord to care for them. They are confident and fearless and can face their foes triumphantly.

—Psalm 112:7-8 NLT

Come to me all you who are weary and burdened, and I will give you rest. Take my yoke upon you and learn from me, for I am gentle and humble in heart, and you will find rest for your soul. For my yoke is easy and my burden is light.

—Matthew 11:28-30 NIV

Wait on the LORD: be of good courage, and he shall strengthen thine heart: wait, I say, on the LORD.

—Psalm 27:14 KJV

From time to time, all of us face adversity. Sometimes, our families must endure losses that leave us breathless. When we face the inevitable difficulties of life, God stands ready to protect us. When we are troubled, we must call upon Him, and, in His own time and according to His own plan, He will heal us.

———

Measure the size of the obstacles against the size of God.

—*Beth Moore*

—A Prayer—

Heavenly Father, You are my strength and my protector. When I am troubled, You comfort me. When I am discouraged, You lift me up. When I am afraid, You deliver me. Let me turn to You, Lord, when I am weak. In times of adversity, let me trust Your plan, and, whatever my circumstances, let me look to You for my strength and my salvation.

—*Amen*

ANGER

Refrain from anger and turn from wrath; do not fret—it leads only to evil.

—Psalm 37:8 NIV

...do not let the sun go down on your anger, and do not give the devil an opportunity.

—Ephesians 4:26-27 NASB

But now ye also put off all these; anger, wrath, malice....

—Colossians 3:8 KJV

A soft answer turneth away wrath: but grievous words stir up anger.

—Proverbs 15:1 KJV

But now faith, hope, love, abide these three; but the greatest of these is love.

—1 Corinthians 13:13 NASB

Motherhood is vastly rewarding, but every mother knows that it can be, at times, frustrating. No family is perfect, and even the most loving mother's patience can, on occasion, wear thin. When you are tempted to lose your temper over the minor inconveniences of life, don't. Turn away from anger, hatred, bitterness and regret. Turn instead to God. He's waiting with open arms…patiently.

———◆———

Peace with God is where all peace begins.

—*Mary Prince*

—A Prayer—

Dear Lord, as a frail human being, I can be quick to anger and slow to forgive. But, I know, Lord, that forgiveness is Your commandment. Let me follow in the footsteps of Your Son Jesus who forgave His persecutors, and, as I turn away from anger, let me claim the peace that You intend for me and my family.

—*Amen*

ASKING GOD

Ask, and it shall be given you; seek, and ye shall find; knock, and it shall be opened unto you: for every one that asketh receiveth; and he that seeketh findeth; and to him that knocketh it shall be opened.

—*Matthew 7:7-8 KJV*

But my God shall supply all your need according to his riches in glory by Christ Jesus.

—*Philippians 4:19 KJV*

"Lord Help!" they cried in their trouble, and he saved them from their distress.

—*Psalm 107:28 NLT*

Come to me all you who are weary and burdened, and I will give you rest. Take my yoke upon you and learn from me, for I am gentle and humble in heart, and you will find rest for your soul. For my yoke is easy and my burden is light.

—*Matthew 11:28-30 NIV*

Are you in need? Ask God to sustain you. Are you troubled? Take your worries to Him in prayer. Are you weary? Seek God's strength. In all things great and small, seek the healing power of God's grace. He hears your prayers, and He will answer.

———※———

Some people think God does not like to be troubled with our constant asking. The way to trouble God is not to come at all.

—*D. L. Moody*

—A Prayer—

Lord, when the demands of the day leave me discouraged, let me turn to You. When I am weak, let me seek Your strength. When I am fearful, Lord, keep me mindful of Your love and Your grace. In all things, let me seek Your will and Your way, today and forever.

—*Amen*

ATTITUDE

Set your mind on the things above, not on the things that are on earth.

—Colossians 3:2 NASB

…the cheerful heart has a continual feast.

—Proverbs 15:15 NIV

Your attitude should be the same as that of Christ Jesus: Who, being in very nature God, did not consider equality with God something to be grasped, but made himself nothing, taking the very nature of a servant, being made in human likeness. And being found in appearance as a man, he humbled himself and became obedient to death—even death on a cross!

—Philippians 2:5-8 NIV

Let the words of my mouth, and the meditations of my heart, be acceptable in thy sight, O Lord, my strength and my redeemer.

—Psalm 19:14 KJV

As Christians, we have every reason to rejoice. God is in His heaven; Christ has risen, and we are the sheep of His flock. Today, as we care for our families, let us count our blessings instead of our hardships. And, let us thank our heavenly Father who is the source of all our blessings.

———

Life is 10% what happens to you, 90% how you respond to it.

—Chuck Swindoll

—A PRAYER—

Dear Lord, let me live my life and love my family with a spirit of optimism and hope. Whatever the circumstances I face, whether good or bad, triumphal or tragic, may my response reflect a Christlike attitude of faith and love for You.

—Amen

THE BIBLE

But he answered and said, It is written, Man shall not live by bread alone but by every word that proceedeth out of the mouth of God.

—*Matthew 4:4 KJV*

The words of the LORD are pure words: as silver tried in a furnace of earth.

—*Psalm 12:6 KJV*

Every word of God is flawless; he is a shield to those who take refuge in him.

—*Proverbs 30:5 NIV*

Whosoever cometh to me, and heareth my sayings, and doeth them, I will show you to whom he is like: he is like a man which built a house, and digged deep, and laid the foundation on a rock: and when the flood arose, the stream beat vehemently upon that house, and could not shake it; for it was founded upon a rock.

—*Luke 6:47-48 KJV*

God has given us the Holy Bible so that we might know His commandments, His wisdom, His love, and His Son. When we study God's teachings, share His Word with our children, and apply His commandments to our daily lives, we live by the Word that shall never pass away.

———

God can see clearly no matter how dark or foggy the night is. Trust His Word to guide you safely home.

—*Lisa Whelchel*

—A Prayer—

Heavenly Father, the Bible is Your gift to me; let me use it and share it with my family. When I stray from Your Holy Word, Lord, I suffer. But, when I place Your Word at the very center of my life, I am blessed. Make me a faithful student of Your Word.

—*Amen*

BLESSINGS

For thou, LORD, wilt bless the righteous....
—Psalm 5:12 KJV

The Lord keeps watch over you as you come and go, both now and forever.
—Psalm 121:8 NLT

The LORD himself goes before you and will be with you; he will never leave you nor forsake you. Do not be afraid; do not be discouraged.
—Deuteronomy 31:8 NIV

But my God shall supply all your need according to his riches in glory by Christ Jesus.
—Philippians 4:19 KJV

...the Lord's unfailing love surrounds the man who trusts in him.
—Psalm 32:10 NIV

God gives us so many blessings that they are too numerous to count. Your blessings include life, family, freedom, friends, talents, and possessions, for starters. But, your greatest blessing—a gift that is yours for the asking—is God's gift of salvation through Christ Jesus. Today, give thanks for your blessings and show your thanks by using them *and* by sharing them.

———

Blessings can either humble us and draw us closer to God, or allow us to become full of pride and self-sufficiency.

—Jim Cymbala

—A Prayer—

Lord, Your blessings are greater than I can imagine. May I live each day with thanksgiving in my heart and praise on my lips. Thank You for the gift of Your Son and for the promise of eternal life. Let me share the joyous news of Jesus Christ with my family and with a world that needs His healing touch this day and every day.

—Amen

CHARACTER

A wife of noble character who can find? She is worth far more than rubies.

—Proverbs 31:10 NIV

Therefore seeing we have this ministry, as we have received mercy, we faint not; but have renounced the hidden things of dishonesty, not walking in craftiness, nor handling the word of God deceitfully; but, by manifestation of the truth, commending ourselves to every man's conscience in the sight of God.

—II Corinthians 4:1 KJV

In everything set them an example by doing what is good. In your teaching show integrity, seriousness and soundness of speech that cannot be condemned, so that those who oppose you may be ashamed because they have nothing bad to say about us.

—Titus 2:7 NIV

Blessed is the man that walketh not in the counsel of the ungodly, nor standeth in the way of sinners, nor sitteth in the seat of the scornful.

—Psalm 1:1 KJV

Wise mothers teach the importance of character. Character is built slowly over a lifetime. It is the sum of every right decision, every honest word, every noble thought, and every heartfelt prayer. It is forged on the anvil of honorable work and polished by the twin virtues of generosity and humility. Character is a precious thing—difficult to build but easy to tear down; godly mothers value it and protect it at all costs...and they encourage their children to do the same.

Character is made in the small moments of our lives.

—Phillips Brooks

—A Prayer—

Lord, let me be a person of integrity. May I be Your worthy servant, and may I live according to Your commandments. May I share Your message with family, friends, and all who cross my path. And, may my words and deeds be a testimony to You, today and always.

—Amen

CHEERFULNESS

This is the day the Lord has made; let us rejoice and be glad in it.

—*Psalm 118:24 NIV*

A merry heart doeth good like a medicine: but a broken spirit drieth the bones.

—*Proverbs 17:22 KJV*

A cheerful look brings joy to the heart, and good news gives health to the bones.

—*Proverbs 15:30 NIV*

The Lord is king! Let the earth rejoice! Let the farthest islands be glad.

—*Psalm 97:1 NLT*

...ye shall be sorrowful, but your sorrow shall be turned into joy.

—*John 16:20 KJV*

All of us, on occasion, have witnessed this sad, sad sight: a grumpy Christian. May we never count ourselves among that number! As believers in Christ, we have countless blessings...so let's spend less time overlooking them and more time counting them...cheerfully.

Joy is available to all who seek His riches. The key to joy is found in the person of Jesus Christ and in His will.

—Kay Arthur

—A PRAYER—

Lord, You have given me many reasons to celebrate. Today, let me choose an attitude of cheerfulness. Let me be a joyful Christian, Lord, quick to laugh and slow to anger. And, let me share Your goodness with my family, my friends, and my neighbors, this day and every day.

—Amen

CHILDREN

And whoever welcomes a little child like this in my name welcomes me. But if anyone causes one of these little ones who believe in me to sin, it would be better for him to have a large milestone hung around his neck and be drowned in the depths of the sea.

—*Matthew 18:5-6 NIV*

Train a child in the way he should go, and when he is old he will not turn from it.

—*Proverbs 22:6 NIV*

My son, hear the instruction of thy father, and forsake not the law of thy mother....

—*Proverbs 1:8 KJV*

And Jesus called a little child unto him, and set him in the midst of them, and said, Verily I say unto you, Except ye be converted, and become as little children, ye shall not enter into the kingdom of heaven.

—*Mathew 18:2-3 KJV*

*E*very child is a priceless gift from the Father above. And, with the Father's gift comes immense responsibility. Wise mothers understand the critical importance of raising their children with love, with family, with discipline, and with God.

———

Do you want to help your children reach the maximum potential that lies within them? Then raise them according to the precepts and values given to us in the Scriptures.

—*James Dobson*

—A Prayer—

*L*ord, You have given me a wonderful responsibility: caring for my children. Let me love them, care for them, nurture them, teach them, and lead them to You. When I am weary, give me strength. When I am frustrated, give me patience. And, let my words and deeds always demonstrate to my children the love that I feel for them...and for You.

—*Amen*

CHRIST'S LOVE

Who shall separate us from the love of Christ? shall tribulation, or distress, or persecution, or famine, or nakedness, or peril, or sword?...Nay, in all these things we are more than conquerors through him that loved us.

—Romans 8:35, 37 KJV

As the Father hath loved me, so have I loved you; continue ye in my love.

—John 15:9 KJV

For I am persuaded, that neither death, nor life, nor angels, nor principalities, nor powers, nor things present, nor things to come, nor height, nor depth, nor any other creature, shall be able to separate us from the love of God, which is in Christ Jesus our Lord.

—Romans 8:38-39 KJV

For God so loved the world that he gave his one and only Son, that whoever believes in him shall not perish but have eternal life.

—John 3:16 NIV

*E*ven though we are imperfect, fallible human beings, even though we have fallen far short of God's commandments, Christ loves us still. His love is perfect and steadfast; it does not waver. May we accept Christ's love, and may we encourage our friends and our families to welcome Him into their hearts.

———❖———

The secret is Christ in me, not me in a different set of circumstances.

—*Elisabeth Elliot*

—A PRAYER—

*T*hank You, Lord, for Your Son. His love is boundless, infinite, and eternal. Let me pause and reflect upon Christ's love for me, and let me share that love with all who come into my life. As an expression of my love for Him, let me share Christ's saving message today and forever.

—*Amen*

Contentment

I know what it is to be in need, and I know what it is to have plenty. I have learned the secret of being content in any and every situation, whether well fed or hungry, whether living in plenty or in want. I can do everything through him who gives me strength.

—Philippians 4:12-13 NIV

Be perfect, be of good comfort, be of one mind, live in peace; and the God of love and peace shall be with you.

—II Corinthians 13:11 KJV

The LORD will give strength to His people; The LORD will bless His people with peace.

—Psalm 29:11 NKJV

Peace I leave with you, my peace I give unto you; not as the world giveth, give I unto you. Let not your heart be troubled, neither let it be afraid.

—John 14:27 KJV

Be still, and know that I am God....

—Psalm 46:10 KJV

Where can we find contentment? Genuine contentment is a gift from God to those who trust in Him and follow His commandments. When God dwells at the center of our families and our lives, contentment will belong to us just as surely as we belong to God.

———◆———

That peace, which has been described, and which believers enjoy, is a participation of the peace which their glorious Lord and Master himself enjoys.

—*Jonathan Edwards*

—A Prayer—

Heavenly Father, You are my contentment. Whatever my circumstances, I find contentment in Your healing hand. Let me look to You, today, Father, for the peace that You have offered me through the gift of Your Son Jesus.

—*Amen*

>>>
COURAGE
>>>

For thou wilt light my candle: the LORD my God will enlighten my darkness.

—Psalm 18:28 KJV

The Lord himself goes before you and will be with you; he will never leave you nor forsake you. Do not be afraid; do not be discouraged.

—Deuteronomy 31:8 NIV

He replied, "You of little faith, why are you so afraid?" Then he got up and rebuked the winds and the waves, and it was completely calm.

—Matthew 8:26 NIV

Fear of man will prove to be a snare, but whoever trusts in the Lord is kept safe.

—Proverbs 29:25 NIV

I sought the LORD, and he heard me, and delivered me from all my fears.

—Psalm 34:4 KJV

*R*aising a family is not easy. Sometimes, the storm clouds form overhead, and we find our faith stretched to the breaking point. As Christians, we can be comforted: Wherever we find ourselves, whether at the top of the mountain or the depths of the valley, God is there. And, because He cares for us, we can live courageously.

———————

If a person fears God, he or she has no reason to fear anything else. On the other hand, if a person does not fear God, then fear becomes a way of life.

—*Beth Moore*

—A PRAYER—

*L*ord, sometimes I face challenges that leave me fearful or discouraged. When I am weary, give me strength. When I am afraid, let me lean upon You. Keep me mindful, Lord, that You are my God, my strength, and my shield. With You by my side, I have nothing to fear. Help me to be a grateful and courageous servant, and help me share Your courage with my family and friends.

—*Amen*

DISCIPLINE

Discipline your son, for in that there is hope....

—*Proverbs 19:18 NIV*

Discipline your son and he will give you peace....

—*Proverbs 29:17 NIV*

The fear of the Lord is the beginning of knowledge, but fools despise wisdom and discipline.

—*Proverbs 1:7 NIV*

He who heeds discipline shows the way to life, but whoever ignores correction leads others astray.

—*Proverbs 10:17 NIV*

Children, obey your parents in all things: for this is well-pleasing unto the Lord.

—*Colossians 3:20 KJV*

*P*arents who study the Bible are confronted again and again with God's intention that His children (of all ages) lead disciplined lives. God does not reward laziness or misbehavior. To the contrary, He expects His own to adopt a disciplined approach to their lives, and He punishes those who disobey His commandments. Wise parents teach discipline by word and by example, but not necessarily in that order.

———

The Bible calls for discipline and a recognition of authority. Children must learn this at home.

—*Billy Graham*

—A Prayer—

*L*ord, let me be a disciplined parent, and let me teach my children to lead disciplined lives. Let me be Your faithful servant, and let me teach faithfulness by my conduct and by my communications. Let me raise up my family in the knowledge of Your Word, Lord, and let me follow Your commandments just as surely as I teach my children to obey You and to love You.

—*Amen*

ENCOURAGEMENT

Do not let any unwholesome talk come out of your mouths, but only what is helpful for building others up according to their needs, that it may benefit those who listen.

—*Ephesians 4:29 NIV*

…provoke not your children to anger, lest they be discouraged.

—*Colossians 3:21 KJV*

Let the word of Christ dwell in you richly in all wisdom; teaching and admonishing one another in psalms and hymns and spiritual songs, singing with grace in your hearts to the Lord.

—*Colossians 3:16 KJV*

Reckless words pierce like a sword, but the tongue of the wise brings healing.

—*Proverbs 12:18 NIV*

Feed the flock of God which is among you….

—*I Peter 5:2 KJV*

*T*hink…pause…then speak: How wise is the mother who can communicate in this fashion. But, all too often, in the rush to have our messages heard, we speak first and think later…with unfortunate results. Today, seek to encourage all who cross your path, especially your family. Measure your words carefully. Speak wisely, not impulsively. Your words will offer encouragement to a family and to a world that can use both.

———

Words. Do you fully understand their power? Can any of us really grasp the mighty force behind the things we say? Do we stop and think before we speak, considering the potency of the words we utter?

—*Joni Eareckson Tada*

—A Prayer—

*D*ear Father, make me an encouraging parent. Just as You have lifted me up, let me also lift up my children in the spirit of encouragement and hope. Today, let me help my children find the strength and the courage to use their gifts according to Your master plan.

—*Amen*

ENERGY

I will lift up mine eyes unto the hills, from which cometh my help.

—Psalm 121:1 KJV

What a help you are to the weak! How you have saved the arm without strength!

—Job 26:2 NASB

For the eyes of the Lord range throughout the earth to strengthen those whose hearts are fully committed to him.

—II Chronicles 16:9 NIV

Cast thy burden upon the Lord, and he shall sustain thee; he shall never suffer the righteous to be moved.

—Psalm 55:22 KJV

…but those who hope in the LORD will renew their strength. They will soar on wings like eagles; they will run and not grow weary, they will walk and not be faint.

—Isaiah 40:31 NIV

If you are a mother with far too many demands and far too few hours in which to meet them, you are not alone. Motherhood is perhaps the world's most demanding profession. But don't fret. Instead, focus upon God and upon His love for you. Then, ask Him for the strength you need to fulfill your responsibilities. God will give you the energy to do the most important things on today's to-do list...*if* you take time to ask Him.

———⊶◦⊷———

God is the One who provides our strength, not only to cope with the demands of the day, but to rise above them. May we look to Him for the strength to soar.

—Mary Prince

—A Prayer—

Lord, let me find my strength in You. When I am weary, give me rest. When I feel overwhelmed, let me look to You for my priorities. Let Your power be my power, Lord, and let Your way be my way, today and forever.

—Amen

ETERNAL LIFE

Jesus answered and said unto her, Whosoever drinketh of this water shall thirst again: but whosoever drinketh of the water that I shall give him shall never thirst; but the water that I shall give him shall be in him a well of water springing up into everlasting life.

—John 4:13-14 KJV

Verily, verily, I say unto you, He that believeth on me hath everlasting life.

—John 6:47 KJV

For if ye live after the flesh, ye shall die: but if ye through the Spirit do mortify the deeds of the body, ye shall live.

—Romans 8:13 KJV

Surely goodness and mercy shall follow me all the days of my life: and I will dwell in the house of the LORD for ever.

—Psalm 23:6 KJV

*C*hrist sacrificed His life on the cross so that we might have eternal life. This gift, freely given from God's only begotten Son, is the priceless possession of everyone who accepts Him as Lord and savior. Claim Christ's gift today.

God loves you and wants you to experience peace and life—abundant and eternal.

—Billy Graham

—A PRAYER—

I know, Lord, this world is not my home; I am only here for a brief while. And, You have given me the priceless gift of eternal life through Your Son Jesus. Keep the hope of heaven fresh in my heart, and, while I am in this world, help me to pass through it with faith in my heart and praise on my lips for You.

—Amen

EVIL

Submit yourselves therefore to God. Resist the devil, and he will flee from you. Draw nigh to God, and he will draw nigh to you.

—*James 4:7-8 KJV*

The wicked say to themselves, "God isn't watching! He will never notice!"

—*Psalm 10:11 NLT*

A fool finds pleasure in evil conduct, but a man of understanding delights in wisdom.

—*Proverbs 10:23 NIV*

Create in me a clean heart, O God; and renew a right spirit within me.

—*Psalm 51:10 KJV*

But now being made free from sin, and become servants to God, ye have your fruit unto holiness, and the end everlasting life. For the wages of sin is death; but the gift of God is eternal life through Jesus Christ our Lord.

—*Romans 6:22-23 KJV*

This world is filled to the brim with temptations that can ensnare us and our children. As wise and caring mothers, we do all that we can to protect our families from the evils of the world. We teach our children by our words and our actions, and then we pray for the best, knowing that the world is a dangerous place but that God is good. And, He has the final word.

———

Of two evils choose neither.

—*C. H. Spurgeon*

—A PRAYER—

Lord, let me be an example of righteousness to my family. Let me teach my children through my words and my deeds. Protect me and my family from the evils of this world so that we might be Your faithful servants forever.

—*Amen*

FAITH

The Lord is my light and my salvation; whom shall I fear? The Lord is the strength of my life; of whom shall I be afraid?

—Psalm 27:1 KJV

Yea, though I walk through the valley of the shadow of death, I will fear no evil: for thou art with me; thy rod and thy staff they comfort me.

—Psalm 23:4 KJV

…I tell you the truth, if you have faith as small as a mustard seed, you can say to this mountain, "Move from here to there" and it will move. Nothing will be impossible for you.

—Matthew 17:20 NIV

…The righteous will live by his faith.

—Habakkuk 2: 4 NIV

But Jesus turned him about, and when he saw her, he said, Daughter, be of good comfort; thy faith hath made thee whole. And the woman was made whole from that hour.

—Matthew 9:22 KJV

When the sun is shining and all is well, it's easy to have faith. When the family is at peace, it is easy to feel at peace, and it is easy to have faith. But, when life takes an unexpected turn for the worse, as it does on occasion, it is easy to lose faith in ourselves and in God. In times of trouble and doubt, God remains faithful to us. We must do the same for Him.

———

Faith is not a feeling; it is action. It is a willed choice.

—Elisabeth Elliot

—A Prayer—

Lord, when this world becomes a fearful place, give me faith. When I am filled with uncertainty and doubt, give me faith. In the dark moments, help me to remember that You can overcome any challenge. And, in the joyous moments, keep me mindful that every gift comes from You. In every aspect of my life, Lord, and in every circumstance, give me faith.

—Amen

FAMILY

He who brings trouble on his family will inherit only wind....

—*Proverbs 11:29 NIV*

Children, obey your parents in all things: for this is well-pleasing unto the Lord.

—*Colossians 3:20 KJV*

Honor your father and your mother, that your days may be prolonged in the land which the LORD your God gives you.

—*Exodus 20:12 NASB*

Listen, my son, to your father's instruction and do not forsake your mother's teaching.

—*Proverbs 1:8 NIV*

Better is a dry morsel and quietness with it than a house full of feasting with strife.

—*Proverbs 17:1 NASB*

Your most prized earthly possession is not your home, your car, or your savings account. Your most prized earthly possession is, of course, your family. Your family is a priceless gift from God. Treasure it, protect it, and dedicate it to Him. When you place God at the center of your family, He will bless you and yours forever.

It matters that we should be true to one another, be loyal to what is a family—only a little family in the great Household, but still a family, with family love alive in it and action as a living bond.

—Amy Carmichael

—A Prayer—

Dear Lord, I am blessed to be part of the family of God where I find love and acceptance. You have also blessed me with my earthly family. May I show the same love and acceptance for my own children that You have shown for me.

—Amen

FEAR

The Lord is my light and my salvation; whom shall I fear? The Lord is the strength of my life; of whom shall I be afraid?

—Psalm 27:1 KJV

Be of good courage, and he shall strengthen your heart, all ye that hope in the Lord.

—Psalm 31:24 KJV

Fear not: for I have redeemed thee, I have called thee by thy name; thou art mine.

—Isaiah 43:1 KJV

...Be strong and courageous. Do not be terrified; do not be discouraged, for the Lord your God will be with you wherever you go.

—Joshua 1:9-10 NIV

He replied, "You of little faith, why are you so afraid?" Then he got up and rebuked the winds and the waves, and it was completely calm.

—Matthew 8:26 NIV

*E*ven dedicated followers of Christ may find their courage tested by the inevitable disappointments and tragedies of life. The next time you find your courage tested, remember that God is as near as your next breath, and remember that He offers salvation to His children. He is your shield and your strength. Call upon Him in your hour of need and be comforted. Whatever the size of your challenge, God is bigger.

———

Do not build up obstacles in your imagination. Difficulties must be studied and dealt with, but they must not be magnified by fear.

—Norman Vincent Peale

—A PRAYER—

*D*ear Lord, when I am fearful, let me seek Your strength. When I am anxious, give me faith. Keep me mindful, Lord, that You are my God and that Your Son Jesus is my Savior. Help me to be Your grateful and courageous servant this day and every day.

—Amen

FORGIVENESS

Blessed are the merciful, for they will be shown mercy.

—Matthew 5:7 NIV

Whenever you stand praying, forgive, if you have anything against anyone, so that your Father in heaven will also forgive you your transgressions.

—Mark 11:24 NASB

He that saith he is in the light, and hateth his brother, is in darkness even until now.

—I John 2:9 KJV

Hatred stirs up dissention, but love covers over all wrongs.

—Proverbs 10:12 NIV

Then came Peter to him, and said, Lord, how oft shall my brother sin against me, and I forgive him? till seven times? Jesus saith unto him, I say not unto thee, Until seven times: but, Until seventy times seven.

—Matthew 18:21-22 KJV

How often must we forgive family members and friends? More times than we can count. Our children are precious but imperfect; so are our spouses and our friends. We must, on occasion, forgive those who have injured us; to do otherwise is to disobey God. If there exists even one person, alive or dead, whom you have not forgiven (and that includes yourself), follow God's commandment and His will for your life: forgive. Hatred and bitterness and regret are not part of God's plan for your life. Forgiveness is.

Forgiveness is not an emotion…. Forgiveness is an act of the will, and the will can function regardless of the temperature of the heart.

—Corrie ten Boom

—A Prayer—

Lord, forgiveness is Your commandment, but sometimes forgiveness is difficult. Help me to forgive those who have injured me, and deliver me from the traps of anger and bitterness. Forgiveness is Your way, Lord; let it be mine.

—Amen

GENEROSITY

Freely you have received, freely give.

—Matthew 10:8 NIV

And above all things have fervent charity among yourselves: for charity shall cover the multitude of sins.

—I Peter 4:8 KJV

Jesus said unto him, Thou shalt love the Lord thy God with all thy heart, and with all thy soul, and with all thy mind. This is the first and great commandment. And the second is like unto it, Thou shalt love thy neighbor as thyself. On these two commandments hang all the law and the prophets.

—Matthew 22:37-40 KJV

He that hath two coats, let him impart to him that hath none; and he that hath meat, let him do likewise.

—Luke 3:11 KJV

As believers in Christ, we are blessed here on earth, and we are blessed eternally through God's grace. We can never fully repay God for His gifts, but we can share them with others. We do so by kindness and generosity to those who enter our lives.

To show great love for God and our neighbor, we need not do great things. It is how much love we put in the doing that makes our offering something beautiful for God.

—*Mother Teresa*

—A Prayer—

Dear Lord, You have been so generous with me; let me be generous with others. Help me to be generous with my time and my possessions as I care for those in need. Help me to teach my children to be cheerful givers, Lord, and make us all humble givers, so that the glory and the praise might be Yours.

—*Amen*

GIFTS

Now there are varieties of gifts, but the same Spirit. And there are varieties of ministries, and the same Lord.

—1 Corinthians 12: 4-5 NASB

Neglect not the gift that is in thee....

—I Timothy 4:14 KJV

Whatever your hand finds to do, do it with all your might....

—Ecclesiastes 9:10 NIV

I can do all things through Him who strengthens me.

—Philippians 4:14 NASB

His lord said unto him, Well done, thou good and faithful servant: thou hast been faithful over a few things, I will make thee ruler over many things: enter thou into the joy of thy lord.

—Matthew 25:21 KJV

Your talents and your children's talents are blessings from God, blessings which must be nurtured. God intends that we all use our talents for the glory of His kingdom. The best way to say "Thank You" for God's gifts is to use them.

———

One thing taught large in the Holy Scriptures is that while God gives His gifts freely, He will require a strict accounting of them at the end of the road. Each of us is personally responsible for his store, be it large or small, and will be required to explain his use of it before the judgment seat of Christ.

—*A. W. Tozer*

—A Prayer—

Heavenly Father, You have blessed me and my family with many talents. Let us discover them, nurture them, and use them to the glory of Your Kingdom. Let us praise You, Lord, and thank You for Your gifts, and let us give all the glory to the Giver of all things good: You.

—*Amen*

GOD'S COMMANDMENTS

Blessed are those whose way is blameless, who walk in the law of the Lord. Blessed are those who keep his testimonies, who seek him with their whole heart.

—Psalm 119:1-2 RSV

Jesus answered and said unto him, If a man love me, he will keep my words: and my Father will love him, and we will come unto him, and make our abode with him.

—John 14:23 KJV

Trust the Lord your God with all your heart and lean not on your own understanding; in all your ways acknowledge him, and he will make your paths straight.

—Proverbs 3:5-6 NIV

For this is the love of God, that we keep his commandments....

—I John 5:3 KJV

A righteous life has many components: faith, honesty, generosity, love, kindness, humility, gratitude, and worship, to name but a few. If we seek to follow the steps of our Savior, Jesus Christ, we must seek to live according to His commandments. In short, we must, to the best of our abilities, live according to the principles contained in God's Holy Word. And, we must teach our children to do the same.

⇒•⇐

We have not learned the commandments until we have learned to do them.

—Vance Havner

—A PRAYER—

Thank You, Heavenly Father, for loving me enough to give me rules to live by. Let me live by Your commandments, and let me lead my children to walk in the paths of righteousness. Let me walk righteously in Your way, Dear Lord, this day and every day.

—Amen

GOD'S GRACE

...for all have sinned and fall short of the glory of God, and are justified freely by his grace through the redemption that came by Christ Jesus.

—*Romans 3:23,24 NIV*

For it is by grace you have been saved, through faith—and this not from yourselves, it is the gift of God—not by works, so that no one can boast.

—*Ephesians 2:8,9 NIV*

As God's fellow workers we urge you not to receive God's grace in vain. For he says, "In the time of my favor I heard you, and in the day of salvation I helped you. I tell you, now is the time of God's favor, now is the day of salvation."

—*II Corinthians 6:1,2 NIV*

Let us then approach the throne of grace with confidence, so that we may receive mercy and find grace to help us in our time of need.

—*Hebrews 4:16 NIV*

We have not earned our salvation; it is a gift from God. When we accept Christ as our savior, we are saved by God's grace. Let us praise God for His gift, and let us share the Good News with our families, our friends, and with all who cross our paths.

———◆———

Grace calls you to get up, throw off your blanket of helplessness, and to move on through life in faith.

—*Kay Arthur*

—A Prayer—

Dear Lord, Your grace is a glorious promise and a priceless gift. You love me, and You save me by grace. Thank You for Your gift, Heavenly Father. Let me share Your love, Your Word, and Your grace with my family and with the world.

—*Amen*

GOD'S LOVE

The Lord is gracious and merciful; slow to anger and great in his lovingkindness. The Lord is good to all, and his mercies are over all his works.

—Psalm 145:8-9 NASB

I will sing of the tender mercies of the Lord forever! Young and old will hear of your faithfulness. Your unfailing love will last forever. Your faithfulness is as enduring as the heavens.

—Psalm 89:1-2 NLT

For God so loved the world, that he gave his only begotten Son, that whosoever believeth in him should not perish, but have everlasting life.

—John 3:16 KJV

The Lord's lovingkindnesses indeed never cease, for His compassions never fail. They are new every morning. Great is Thy faithfulness.

—Lamentations 3:22-23 NASB

$\mathcal{G}$od is a loving Father. We are God's children, and we are called upon to be faithful to Him. We return our Father's love by sharing it with others. We honor our Heavenly Father by obeying His commandments and sharing His message. When we do, we are blessed…and the Father smiles.

———

God carries your picture in his wallet.

—*Tony Campolo*

—A PRAYER—

$\mathcal{T}$hank You, Lord, for Your love. Your love is boundless, infinite, and eternal. Today, let me pause and reflect upon Your love for me, and let me share that love with my family, my neighbors, and with everyone I meet.

—*Amen*

GOD'S PLAN

The Lord will work out his plans for my life—
for your faithful love, O Lord, endures forever.

—Psalm 138:8 NLT

For every house is built by someone, but the
builder of all things is God.

—Hebrews 3:4 NASB

There is no wisdom, no insight, no plan that
can succeed against the Lord.

—Proverbs 21:30 NIV

In his heart a man plans his course, but the
Lord determines his steps.

—Proverbs 16:9 NIV

The steps of a good man are ordered by the
LORD....

—Psalm 37:23 KJV

God has plans for you and your family, but He won't force those plans upon you. God has given you free will. You and your family possess the ability to make choices, and when you make them, you must live with the consequences of those choices. God intends to use you in wonderful, unexpected ways, and he seeks to do the same for your children. Seek God's plan for your life, and encourage your family to do the same. God's plans are grand and glorious…more glorious than you can imagine.

———

Every experience God gives us, every person he puts in our lives, is the perfect preparation for the future that only he can see.

—Corrie ten Boom

—A Prayer—

Dear Lord, let me choose Your plans. You created me, and You have called me to do Your work here on earth. Today, I choose to seek Your will and to live it, knowing that when I trust in You, I am eternally blessed.

—Amen

God's Support

Come unto me, all ye that labor and are heavy laden, and I will give you rest.

—*Matthew 11:28 KJV*

For I the LORD thy God will hold thy right hand, saying unto thee, Fear not; I will help thee.

—*Isaiah 41:13 KJV*

Seek the LORD, and his strength: seek his face evermore. Remember his marvelous works....

—*Psalm 105:4-5 KJV*

The Lord is my rock, my fortress and my savior; my God is my rock in whom I find protection. He is my shield, the strength of my salvation, and my stronghold.

—*Psalm 18:2 NLT*

The Lord is my shepherd; I shall not want.

—*Psalm 23:1 KJV*

*M*others know that life is not always easy. But, godly mothers also know that they are protected by a loving God. In times of trouble, God comforts us; in times of sorrow, He dries our tears. When we are troubled, or weak, or sorrowful, God is as near as our next breath. Let us build our lives on the rock that cannot be shaken…let us trust in God.

———————

In God's faithfulness lies eternal security.
—Corrie ten Boom

—A PRAYER—

*D*ear Lord, You never leave me or forsake me. You are always with me, protecting me and encouraging me. Whatever this day may bring, I thank You for Your love and Your strength. Let me lean upon You, Father, this day and forever.

—Amen

>>>
God's Timing
>>>

He has made everything beautiful in its time.
He has also set eternity in the hearts of men; yet
they cannot fathom what God has done from beginning to end.

—Ecclesiastes 3:11 NIV

Wait for the LORD; be strong and take heart
and wait for the LORD.

—Psalm 27:14 NIV

He said to them: "It is not for you to know
the times or dates the Father has set by his own
authority."

—Acts 1:7 NIV

The steps of the Godly are directed by the
Lord. He delights in every detail of their lives.
Though they stumble, they will not fall, for the
Lord holds them by the hand.

—Psalm 37:23-24 NLT

I waited patiently for the LORD; And He
inclined to me, And heard my cry.

—Psalm 40:1 NKJV

As fallible human beings, we are impatient. We know what we want, and we know exactly when we want it: NOW! But, God knows better. He has created a world that unfolds according to His own timetable, not ours. Let us be patient, and let us teach our children to do likewise. In His own time, God will reveal the glorious plans that He has for our lives.

...when we read of the great biblical leaders, we see that it was not uncommon for God to ask them to wait, not just a day or two, but for years until God was ready for them to act.

—*Gloria Gaither*

—A Prayer—

Dear Lord, You have a plan for my life, and Your timing is always right for me. When I am impatient, remind me that You are never early or late. You are always on time, Lord, so let me trust in You...always.

—*Amen*

GOLDEN RULE

Therefore all things whatsoever ye would that men should do to you, do ye even so to them: for this is the law and the prophets.

—*Matthew 7:12 KJV*

As we have therefore opportunity, let us do good unto all men, especially unto them who are of the household of faith.

—*Galatians 6:10 KJV*

Be ye therefore merciful, as your Father also is merciful.

—*Luke 6:36 KJV*

Be gentle unto all men, apt to teach, patient.

—*II Timothy 2:24 KJV*

God is love; and he that dwelleth in love dwelleth in God, and God in him.

—*I John 4:16 KJV*

All over the world, loving mothers teach the same lesson: kindness. Christ taught this message when He spoke the words recorded in *Matthew 7:12*. The Golden Rule commands us to treat others as we wish to be treated. When we weave the thread of kindness into the very fabric of our lives, we give glory to the One who gave His life for us.

If my heart is right with God, every human being is my neighbor.

—*Oswald Chambers*

—A PRAYER—

Dear Lord, the Golden Rule is not only a perfect standard to use with my friends and neighbors, it is also a guide for raising my children. Enable me to respect my children as I want them to respect me. Help me to walk in their shoes and to see life from their perspective. Help me to be a nurturing, loving mother every day that I live, and may the glory be Yours.

—*Amen*

GRATITUDE

Enter his gates with thanksgiving, go into his courts with praise. Give thanks to him and bless his name.

—*Psalm 100:4 NLT*

It is a good thing to give thanks unto the LORD, and to sing praises unto thy name, O Most High....

—*Psalm 92:1 KJV*

...in all your ways acknowledge him, and he will make your paths straight.

—*Proverbs 3:6 NIV*

Rejoice evermore. Pray without ceasing. In every thing give thanks: for this is the will of God in Christ Jesus concerning you.

—*I Thessalonians 5:16-18 KJV*

Delight thyself also in the LORD; and he shall give thee the desires of thine heart.

—*Psalm 37:4 KJV*

We teach our children to say "please" and "thank you." And, as adults, we should approach God in the same way. We should offer up our needs to Him in prayer ("Please, Dear Lord…."), and we should always say "Thank You" for the gifts He has given us. Let us praise God and thank Him. He is the Giver of all things good.

———◆———

It is only with gratitude that life becomes rich.

—*Dietrich Bonhoeffer*

—A PRAYER—

Dear Lord, I want my attitude to be one of gratitude. You have given me much; when I think of Your grace and Your goodness to me, I am humbled and thankful. Let me express my gratitude not just through my words but also through my deeds. Make me a grateful Christian, Lord, today and forever.

—*Amen*

GRIEF

Blessed are those who mourn, for they will be comforted.

—Matthew 5:4 NIV

They that sow in tears shall reap in joy.

—Psalm 126:5 KJV

...but we glory in tribulations also; knowing that tribulation worketh patience; and patience, experience; and experience, hope....

—Romans 5:3-4 KJV

For thou wilt light my candle: the LORD my God will enlighten my darkness.

—Psalm 18:28 KJV

Then spake Jesus again unto them, saying, I am the light of the world: he that followeth me shall not walk in darkness, but shall have the light of life.

—John 8:12 KJV

All of us experience adversity and pain. When we lose something—or someone—we love, we grieve our losses. During times of heartache, we can turn to God for solace. When we do, He comforts us and, in time, He heals us.

⟶◆⟵

The grace of God is sufficient for all our needs, for every problem and for every difficulty, for every broken heart, and for every human sorrow.

—Peter Marshall

—A Prayer—

You have promised, Lord, that You will never give me burdens that are greater than I can bear. You have promised to lift me up out of my grief and despair. You have promised that, in time, I will laugh again. I thank You, Lord, for sustaining me in my day of sorrow. Restore me, and heal me, and use me as You will.

—Amen

HOPE

Be of good courage, and he shall strengthen your heart, all ye that hope in the Lord.

—*Psalm 31:24 KJV*

…those who hope in the Lord will inherit the land.

—*Psalm 37:9 NIV*

Now faith is the substance of things hoped for, the evidence of things not seen.

—*Hebrews 11:1 KJV*

I will lift up mine eyes unto the hills, from whence cometh my help. My help cometh from the Lord, which made heaven and earth.

—*Psalm 121:1-2 KJV*

For we are saved by hope….

—*Romans 8:24 KJV*

This world can be a place of trials and tribulations, but as believers we are secure. We need never lose hope, because God has promised us peace, joy, and eternal life. So, let us face each day with hope in our hearts and trust in our God. And, let us teach our children to do likewise. After all, God has promised us that we are His throughout eternity, and he keeps His promises.

———

Hope is no other than the expectation of those things which faith has believed to be truly promised by God.

—John Calvin

—A Prayer—

Lord, when my heart is troubled, let me trust in You. When I become discouraged, let me depend upon You. When I lose faith in this world, let me hold tightly to my faith in You. Remind me, Lord, that in every situation and in every season of life, You will love me and protect me. You are my strength, Lord, and I need never lose hope because You remain sovereign today and forever.

—Amen

JESUS

The next day John seeth Jesus coming unto him, and saith, Behold the Lamb of God, which taketh away the sin of the world!

—John 1:29 KJV

Jesus saith unto him, I am the way, the truth, and the life: no man cometh unto the Father, but by me. If ye had known me, ye should have known my Father also: and from henceforth ye know him, and have seen him.

—John 14:6-7 KJV

For I am persuaded, that neither death, nor life, nor angels, nor principalities, nor powers, nor things present, nor things to come, nor height, nor depth, nor any other creature, shall be able to separate us from the love of God, which is in Christ Jesus our Lord.

—Romans 8:38-39 KJV

For the Son of man is come to save that which was lost.

—Matthew 18:11 KJV

The old familiar hymn begins, "What a friend we have in Jesus…." No truer words were ever penned. Jesus is the sovereign friend and ultimate savior of mankind. Christ showed enduring love for His believers by willingly sacrificing His own life so that we might have eternal life. Let us love Him, praise Him, and share His message of salvation with our families, with our friends, and with the world.

———⋙•◦•⋘———

The secret of the Christian is that he knows the absolute deity of the Lord Jesus Christ.

—*Oswald Chambers*

—A PRAYER—

Thank You, Lord, for Your Son Jesus, the Savior of my life. You loved this world so dearly, Lord, that You sent Your Son to die so that we, Your children, might have life eternal. Let the love of Jesus be reflected in my words, my thoughts, and my deeds. Let me always count Jesus as my dearest friend, and let me share His transforming message with a world in desperate need of His peace.

—*Amen*

JOY

This is the day which the Lord hath made; we will rejoice and be glad in it.

—Psalm 118:24 KJV

I will thank you, Lord with all my heart; I will tell of all the marvelous things you have done. I will be filled with joy because of you. I will sing praises to your name, O Most High.

—Psalm 9:1-2 NLT

...these things I speak in the world, that they might have my joy fulfilled in themselves.

—John 17:13 KJV

I will praise the name of God with a song, and will magnify him with thanksgiving.

—Psalm 69:30 KJV

And let the peace of God rule in your hearts...and be ye thankful.

—Colossians 3:15 KJV

Christ made it clear to His followers: He intended that His joy would become their joy. And it still holds true today: Christ intends that His believers share His love and His joy. Let the joy of Christ into your heart and share it freely with family and friends, just as Christ freely shared His joy with you.

Claim the joy that is yours. Pray. And know that your joy is used by God to reach others.

—*Kay Arthur*

—A Prayer—

Dear Lord, You have created a glorious universe that is far beyond my understanding. You have given me the gift of Your Son and the gift of salvation. Let me be a joyful Christian, Lord, this day and every day. Today is Your gift to me. Let me use it to Your glory while giving all the praise to You.

—*Amen*

JUDGING OTHERS

Judge not, and ye shall not be judged: condemn not, and ye shall not be condemned: forgive, and ye shall be forgiven....

—Luke 6:37 KJV

Therefore no one is to act as your judge in regard to food or drink or in respect to a festival or a new moon or a Sabbath day....

—Colossians 2:16 NASB

Either how canst thou say to thy brother, Brother, let me pull out the mote that is in thine eye, when thou thyself beholdest not the beam that is in thine own eye? Thou hypocrite, cast out first the beam out of thine own eye, and then shalt thou see clearly to pull out the mote that is in thy brother's eye.

—Luke 6:42 KJV

Therefore judge nothing before the time, until the Lord come, who both will bring to light the hidden things of darkness, and will make manifest the counsels of the hearts: and then shall every man have praise of God.

—I Corinthians 4:5 KJV

We have all fallen short of God's commandments, and He has forgiven us. We, too, must forgive others. And we must refrain from judging them. As Christian believers, we are warned that to judge others is to invite fearful consequences: to the extent we judge others, so, too, will we be judged by God. Let us refrain, then, from judging our neighbors. Instead, let us forgive them and love them in the same way that God has forgiven us.

———

Only the truly forgiven are truly forgiving.

—*C. S. Lewis*

—A PRAYER—

Heavenly Father, sometimes I am quick to judge others. But, You have commanded me not to judge. Keep me mindful, Lord, that when I judge others, I am living outside of Your will for my life. You have forgiven me, Lord. Let me forgive others, let me love them, and let me help them...without judging them.

—*Amen*

KINDNESS

A kind man benefits himself, but a cruel man brings trouble on himself.

—Proverbs 11:17 NIV

A gentle answer turns away wrath, but a harsh word stirs up anger.

—Proverbs 15:1 NIV

…Verily I say unto you, Inasmuch as ye have done it unto one of the least of these my brethren, ye have done it unto me.

—Matthew 25:40 KJV

Be kindly affectioned one to another with brotherly love; in honor preferring one another; not slothful in business; fervent in spirit; serving the Lord; rejoicing in hope; patient in tribulation; continuing instant in prayer….

—Romans 12:10-12 KJV

A new commandment I give unto you, That ye love one another; as I have loved you….

—John 13:34 KJV

If we are to follow the commands of our Lord and savior, we must sow seeds of kindness wherever we go. Kindness is God's way. So, today, let's be a little kinder than necessary, and let's teach our children the art of kindness through our words and our deeds. Our children are watching...and so is God.

———◆———

The nicest thing we can do for our heavenly Father is to be kind to one of His children.

—*St. Teresa of Avila*

—A Prayer—

Help me, Lord, to meet the needs of my family and friends. Today, let me spread words of hope and celebration in honor of Your Son. Today, let forgiveness rule my heart. And every day, Lord, let my love for Christ be reflected through deeds of kindness for those who need the healing touch of the Master's hand.

—*Amen*

KNOWLEDGE

By wisdom a house is built, and through understanding it is established; through knowledge its rooms are filled with rare and beautiful treasures.

—Proverbs 24:3-4 NIV

The fear of the Lord is the beginning of knowledge, but fools despise wisdom and discipline.

—Proverbs 1:7 NIV

Teach me, O Lord, the way of Thy statutes, and I shall observe it to the end.

—Psalm 119:33 NASB

The fear of the Lord is the beginning of wisdom: a good understanding have all they that do his commandments: his praise endureth for ever.

—Psalm 111:10 KJV

Trust in the LORD with all thine heart; and lean not unto thine own understanding. In all thy ways acknowledge him, and he shall direct thy paths.

—Proverbs 3:5-6 KJV

Our children need both knowledge and wisdom. Knowledge is found in textbooks. Wisdom, on the other hand, is found in God's Holy Word and in the carefully-chosen words of loving parents and thoughtful teachers. When we give our children the gift of knowledge, we do them a wonderful service. But, when we share the gift of wisdom, we offer a timeless treasure that surpasses knowledge and reshapes eternity.

———»•«———

Knowledge is horizontal. Wisdom is vertical. It comes down from above.

—*Billy Graham*

—A Prayer—

Lord, help me to be a parent who values both education and wisdom. Let me teach my children what to know *and* how to live. Let me speak words of wisdom, Lord, and more importantly, let me live wisely so that I might be a worthy example to my children every day that I live.

—*Amen*

LAUGHTER

A cheerful heart is good medicine....

—*Proverbs 17:22 NIV*

There is a time for everything, and a season for every activity under heaven...a time to weep and a time to laugh, a time to mourn and a time to dance.

—*Ecclesiastes 3:1,4 NIV*

Thou wilt show me the path of life: in thy presence is fulness of joy; at thy right hand there are pleasures for evermore.

—*Psalm 16:11 KJV*

This is the day which the Lord hath made; we will rejoice and be glad in it.

—*Psalm 118:24 KJV*

...let the hearts of those who seek the Lord rejoice.

—*I Chronicles 16:10-11 NIV*

It has been said, quite correctly, that laughter is a priceless gift from God. Today, as you go about your daily activities, whether at work or at home, approach life with a smile on your face and a chuckle on your lips. After all, God created laughter for a reason...a very *good* reason.

———•———

Laughter dulls the sharpest pain and flattens out the greatest stress. To share it is to give a gift of health.

—Barbara Johnson

—A PRAYER—

Heavenly Father, when I begin to take myself or my life too seriously, let me laugh. When I rush from place to place, slow me down, Lord, and let me laugh. Put a smile on my face and let me share that smile with family and friends...and let me laugh.

—Amen

LOVING GOD

He that loveth not, knoweth not God; for God is love.

—I John 4:8 KJV

Jesus replied, "'Love the Lord your God with all your heart and with all your soul and with all your mind.' This is the first and greatest commandment. And the second is like it: 'Love your neighbor as yourself.' All the Law and the Prophets hang on these two commandments."

—Matthew 22:37-40 NIV

For this is the love of God, that we keep his commandments....

—I John 5:3 KJV

I will thank you, Lord with all my heart; I will tell of all the marvelous things you have done. I will be filled with joy because of you. I will sing praises to your name, O Most High.

—Psalm 9:1-2 NLT

We love him, because he first loved us.

—I John 4:19 KJV

C. S. Lewis observed, "A man's spiritual health is exactly proportional to his love for God." If we are to enjoy the spiritual health that God intends for our lives, we must praise Him and Love Him. And, this is as it should be; after all, He first loved us.

———◦◦◦———

…when an honest soul can get still before the living Christ, we can still hear Him say simply and clearly, "Love the Lord you God with all your heart and with all your soul and with all your mind….and love one another as I have loved you."

—*Gloria Gaither*

—A Prayer—

Dear Heavenly Father, You have blessed me and my family with a love that is infinite and eternal. May we love You, Lord, more and more each day. Make me a worthy parent and a loving servant, Dear Lord. And, let me show my love for You by sharing Your message and Your love with my family and with the world.

—*Amen*

LOVING OTHERS

But now faith, hope, love, abide these three; but the greatest of these is love.

—*1 Corinthians 13:13 NASB*

He that loveth his brother abideth in the light, and there is none occasion of stumbling in him.

—*I John 2:10 KJV*

Hatred stirs up dissention, but love covers over all wrongs.

—*Proverbs 10:12 NIV*

A new commandment I give unto you, That ye love one another; as I have loved you....

—*John 13:34 KJV*

God is love; and he that dwelleth in love dwelleth in God, and God in him.

—*I John 4:16 KJV*

The familiar words of *1st Corinthians 13* remind us that love is God's commandment. Faith is important, of course. So too is hope. But, love is more important still. Christ showed His love for us on the cross, and, as Christians, we are called upon to return Christ's love by sharing it. Today, let us spread Christ's love to families, friends, *and* strangers by word and by deed.

You always win a better response with love.
—Helen Hosier

—A Prayer—

Lord, You have given me the gift of everlasting love; let me share that gift with my family and my friends. Make me generous, Lord, with words of encouragement. And, help me always to reflect the love that Christ Jesus gave me so that through me, others might find Him.
—Amen

MARRIAGE

Who can find a virtuous woman? For her price is far above rubies.

—*Proverbs 31:10 KJV*

Nevertheless, let every one of you in particular so love his wife even as himself; and the wife see that she reverence her husband.

—*Ephesians 5:33 KJV*

A virtuous woman is a crown to her husband....

—*Proverbs 12:4 KJV*

Let love and faithfulness never leave you ...write them on the tablet of your heart.

—*Proverbs 3:3 NIV*

If I have *the gift of* prophecy, and know all mysteries and all knowledge; and if I have all faith, so as to remove mountains, but do not have love, I am nothing.

—*1 Corinthians 13:2 NASB*

A healthy marriage is an exercise in love, fidelity, trust, understanding, forgiveness, caring, sharing, and encouragement. It requires empathy, tenderness, patience, and perseverance. It is the union of two adults, both of whom are willing to compromise and, when appropriate, to apologize. It requires heaping helpings of common sense, common courtesy, and uncommon caring. A healthy marriage is a joy to behold, an even greater joy to experience…and a blessing forever.

———

True love is spelled G-I-V-E. It is not based on what you can get, but rooted in what you can give to the other person.

—Josh McDowell

—A Prayer—

Lord, love is Your commandment. Help me always to remember that the gift of love is a precious gift indeed. Let me nurture love and treasure it. And, keep me mindful that the essence of love is not receiving, it is giving.

—Amen

MIRACLES

And Jesus looking upon them saith, With men it is impossible, but not with God: for with God all things are possible.

—*Mark 10:27 KJV*

Let every soul be subject unto the higher powers. For there is no power but of God: the powers that be are ordained of God.

—*Romans 13:1 KJV*

Search for the Lord and for his strength, and keep on searching. Think of the wonderful works he has done, the miracles and the judgments he handed down.

—*Psalm 105:4-5 NLT*

…Be strong and courageous. Do not be terrified; do not be discouraged, for the Lord your God will be with you wherever you go.

—*Joshua 1:9-10 NIV*

Is anything too hard for the Lord?

—*Genesis 18:14 KJV*

Sometimes, because we are imperfect human beings with limited understanding and limited faith, we place limitations on God. But God's power has no limitations. God will work miracles in our lives *if* we trust Him with everything we have and everything we are. When we do, we will experience the miraculous results of His endless love and His awesome power.

———

We have a God who delights in impossibilities.
—*Andrew Murray*

—A PRAYER—

Heavenly Father, Your infinite power is beyond human understanding. With You, Lord, nothing is impossible. Keep me always mindful of Your power. When I lose hope, give me faith; when others lose hope, let me tell them of Your glory and Your works. Today, Lord, let me expect the miraculous, and let me trust in You.

—*Amen*

MISSIONS

You are the light of the world. A city on a hill cannot be hidden. Neither do people light a lamp and put it under a bowl. Instead they put it on its stand, and it gives light to everyone in the house. In the same way, let your light shine before men, that they may see your good deeds and praise your Father in heaven.

—Matthew 5:14-16 NIV

The fruit of the righteous is a tree of life; and he that winneth souls is wise.

—Proverbs 11:30 KJV

And Jesus said unto them, Come ye after me, and I will make you to become fishers of men. And straightway they forsook their nets, and followed him.

—Mark 1:17-18 KJV

Now then we are ambassadors for Christ....

—II Corinthians 5:20 KJV

As believers, we are called to share the Good News of Jesus Christ with our families, our neighbors, and the world. Jesus commanded His disciples to become fishers of men. We must do likewise. And, the time to go fishing is now.

———✦———

You can go to the mission field in person, by prayer, by provision, or by proxy. But remember, there is a mission field across the street as well as across the sea.

—Vance Havner

—A Prayer—

Heavenly Father, every man and woman, every boy and girl is Your child. You desire that all Your children know Jesus as their Lord and Savior. Father, let me be part of Your Great Commission. Let me give, let me pray, and let me go out into this world so that I might be a fisher of men...for You.

—Amen

MISTAKES

Have mercy on me, O God, according to your unfailing love; according to your great compassion blot out my transgressions. Wash away all my iniquity and cleanse me from my sin.

—*Psalm 51:1,2 NIV*

If we confess our sins, he is faithful and just and will forgive us our sins and purify us from all unrighteousness.

—*1 John 1:9 NIV*

He who conceals his sins does not prosper, but whoever confesses and renounces them finds mercy.

—*Proverbs 28:13 NIV*

I waited patiently for the LORD; he turned to me and heard my cry. He lifted me out of...the mud and mire; he set my feet on a rock and gave me a firm place to stand. He put a new song in my mouth, a hymn of praise to our God....

—*Psalm 40:1-3 NIV*

As parents, we are far from perfect. And, without question, our children are imperfect as well. Thus, we are imperfect parents raising imperfect children, and, as a result, mistakes are bound to happen. When *we* make mistakes, we must correct them and learn from them. And, when *our children* make mistakes, we must help them do likewise. Finally, we must forgive our children, just as our heavenly Father has forgiven us.

———

Lord, when we are wrong, make us willing to change; and when we are right, make us easy to live with.

—*Peter Marshall*

—A Prayer—

Heavenly Father, I am imperfect, and I fail You in many ways. Thank You for Your forgiveness. When my children fall short of Your commandments, Lord, let me love them, let me correct them, and let me forgive them just as You have forgiven them…and me.

—*Amen*

OBEDIENCE

It is the LORD your God you must follow, and him you must revere. Keep his commands and obey him; serve him and hold fast to him.

—Deuteronomy 13:4 NIV

Teach me, O LORD, to follow your decrees; then I will keep them to the end. Give me understanding, and I will keep your law and obey it with all my heart.

—Psalm 119:33,34 NIV

Jesus replied, "If anyone loves me, he will obey my teaching. My Father will love him, and we will come to him and make our home with him."

—John 14:23 NIV

But if anyone obeys his word, God's love is truly made complete in him. This is how we know we are in him: Whoever claims to live in him must walk as Jesus did.

—1 John 2:5,6 NIV

God has given us the Holy Bible as a guidebook for righteous living. It contains thorough instructions which, if followed, lead to fulfillment, righteousness and salvation. But, if we choose to ignore God's commandments, the results are as predictable as they are tragic. Let us walk with God and obey His teachings. Then, let us teach our children to follow in our footsteps...and His.

———————

Our obedience does not make God any bigger or better than He already is.... Anything God commands of us is so that our joy may be full—the joy of seeing His glory revealed to us and in us!

—Beth Moore

—A Prayer—

Heavenly Father, when I turn my thoughts away from You and Your Word, I suffer. But when I obey Your commandments, when I place my faith in You, I am safe. Let me live according to Your commandments. Let me discover Your will and follow it, Dear Lord, this day and always.

—Amen

OPTIMISM

I can do everything through him that gives me strength.

—Philippians 4:13 NIV

The Lord is my light and my salvation; whom shall I fear? The Lord is the strength of my life; of whom shall I be afraid?

—Psalm 27:1 KJV

These things have I spoken unto you, that my joy might remain in you, and that your joy might be full.

—John 15:11 KJV

Finally, brethren, whatsoever things are true, whatsoever things are honest, whatsoever things are just, whatsoever things are pure, whatsoever things are lovely, whatsoever things are of good report; if there be any virtue, and if there be any praise, think on these things.

—Philippians 4:8 KJV

As Christians, we have every reason to think optimistically. As John Calvin observed, "There is not one blade of grass, there is no color in this world that is not intended to make us rejoice." Today, think optimistically about yourself and your world. Then, share your optimism with your children. You'll be better for it...and so will they.

———◦———

At least ten times every day, affirm this thought: "I expect the best and, with God's help, will attain the best."

—Norman Vincent Peale

—A Prayer—

Lord, let me be an expectant Christian. Let me expect the best from You, and let me look for the best in others. If I become discouraged, Lord, turn my thoughts and my prayers to You. Let me trust You, Lord, to direct my life. And, let me be Your faithful, hopeful, optimistic servant every day that I live.

—Amen

PARENTING

Train up a child in the way he should go: and when he is old, he will not depart from it.

—Proverbs 22:6 KJV

...do not provoke your children to anger, but bring them up in the discipline and instruction of the Lord.

—Ephesians 6:4 NASB

Withhold not correction from the child....

—Proverbs 23:13 KJV

Every kingdom divided against itself will be ruined, and every city or household divided against itself will not stand.

—Matthew 12:25 NIV

But now faith, hope, love, abide these three; but the greatest of these is love.

—1 Corinthians 13:13 NASB

*P*arenting is a full-time job with great responsibilities and the potential for even greater rewards. Our challenge, as parents, is to raise our children lovingly, responsibly, and according to God's commandments. When we do, the difficult job of parenting is made easier, and our families are forever blessed.

———◦❖◦———

The balance of affirmation and discipline, freedom and restraint, encouragement and warning is different for each child and season and generation, yet the absolutes of God's Word are necessary and trustworthy at all times.

—Gloria Gaither

—A PRAYER—

*D*ear Lord, help me to be a responsible, loving, godly parent. Let me teach my children to worship You and to study Your Holy Word. When I am uncertain, Lord, give me wisdom. And, in everything that I do and say, let me be a worthy example to my family every day that I live.

—Amen

PATIENCE

And we desire that each one of you show the same diligence so as to realize the full assurance of hope until the end, so that you will not be sluggish, but imitators of those who through faith and patience inherit the promises.

—*Hebrews 6:11-12 NASB*

Better a patient man than a warrior, a man who controls his temper than one who takes a city.

—*Proverbs 16:32 NIV*

Wait on the LORD: be of good courage, and he shall strengthen thine heart: wait, I say, on the LORD.

—*Psalm 27:14 KJV*

…Those who wait upon the Lord, they shall inherit the earth.

—*Psalm 37:9 KJV*

We urge you, brethren, admonish the unruly, encourage the fainthearted, help the weak, be patient with everyone.

—*I Thessalonians 5:14 NASB*

*P*arenting requires patience. From time to time, even the most mannerly children may do things that worry us, or confuse us, or anger us. Why? Because they are children and because they are human. And, it is precisely *because* they are human that we must, from time to time, be patient with our children's shortcomings (just as they, too, must be patient with ours). Sometimes, patience is the price we pay for being responsible parents. After all, think how patient our heavenly Father has been with us.

Patience is the companion of wisdom.

—*St. Augustine*

—A PRAYER—

*H*eavenly Father, give me patience. When I am hurried, slow me down. When I become impatient with others, give me empathy. When I am frustrated by the demands of the day, give me peace. Today, let me be a patient Christian, Dear Lord, as I trust in You and in Your master plan for my life.

—*Amen*

>>>

PEACE

>>>

Be perfect, be of good comfort, be of one mind, live in peace; and the God of love and peace shall be with you.

—II Corinthians 13:11 KJV

Come to me all you who are weary and burdened, and I will give you rest. Take my yoke upon you and learn from me, for I am gentle and humble in heart, and you will find rest for your soul. For my yoke is easy and my burden is light.

—Matthew 11:28-30 NIV

Peace I leave with you, my peace I give unto you: not as the world giveth, give I unto you. Let not your heart be troubled, neither let it be afraid.

—John 14:27 KJV

And let the peace of God rule in your hearts...and be ye thankful.

—Colossians 3:15 KJV

The timeless words of *John 14:27* give us hope: Jesus offers us peace, not as the world gives, but as He alone gives. We, as believers, can accept His peace, and when we do, we are transformed. Today, as a gift to yourself, to your family, and to your friends, claim the inner peace that is your spiritual birthright: the peace of Jesus Christ. It is offered freely; it has been paid for in full; it is yours for the asking. So ask. And then share.

———◆———

Peace is full confidence that God is Who He says He is and that He will keep every promise in His Word.

—Dorothy Harrison Pentecost

—A PRAYER—

Lord, when I turn my thoughts and prayers to You, I feel the peace that You intend for my life. But sometimes, Lord, I am distracted by the busyness of the day or the demands of the moment. Today, help me to trust Your will, to follow Your commands, and to accept Your peace.

—Amen

PERSEVERANCE

For you have need of endurance, so that when you have done the will of God, you may receive what was promised.

—*Hebrews 10:36 NASB*

…I do not consider myself yet to have taken hold of it. But one thing I do: Forgetting what is behind and straining toward what is ahead, I press on toward the goal to win the prize for which God has called me heavenward in Christ Jesus.

—*Philippians 3:13-14 NIV*

Give your burdens to the Lord, and he will take care of you. He will not permit the Godly to slip and fall.

—*Psalm 55:22 NLT*

…but those who hope in the LORD will renew their strength. They will soar on wings like eagles; they will run and not grow weary, they will walk and not be faint.

—*Isaiah 40:31 NIV*

Someone once said, "Life is a marathon, not a sprint." The same can be said for motherhood. Motherhood requires courage, perseverance, determination, and, of course, an unending supply of motherly love. Are you tired? Ask God for strength. Are you discouraged? Believe in His promises. Are you frustrated or fearful? Pray as if everything depended upon God, and work as if everything depended upon you. With God's help, you will find the strength to be the kind of mother that makes her heavenly Father beam with pride.

———※———

Let us not cease to do the utmost, that we may incessantly go forward in the way of the Lord.

—*John Calvin*

—A PRAYER—

Dear Lord, when the pace of my life becomes frantic, slow me down and give me perspective. Keep me steady and sure. When I become weary, let me persevere so that, in Your time, I might finish my work here on earth, and that You might then say, "Well done my good and faithful servant."

—*Amen*

POSSESSIONS

Lay not up for yourselves treasures upon earth, where moth and rust doth corrupt, and where thieves break through and steal: but lay up for yourselves treasures in heaven, where neither moth nor rust doth corrupt, and where thieves do not break through nor steal: for where your treasure is, there will your heart be also.

—*Matthew 6:19-21 KJV*

Whoever loves money never has money enough; whoever loves wealth is never satisfied with his income.

—*Ecclesiastes 5:10 NIV*

Therefore I say unto you, Take no thought for your life, what ye shall eat, or what ye shall drink; nor yet for your body, what ye shall put on. Is not the life more than meat, and the body than raiment? Behold the fowls of the air: for they sow not, neither do they reap, nor gather into barns; yet your heavenly Father feedeth them. Are ye not much better than they?

—*Matthew 6:25-26 KJV*

On the grand stage of a well-lived life, material possessions should play a rather small role. Of course we all need the basic necessities of life, but once we meet those needs for ourselves and for our families, the piling up of possessions creates more problems than it solves. Our real riches are not of this world. In fact, we are never really rich *until* we are rich in spirit.

———◈———

What we possess often possesses us—we are possessed by possessions.

—*Oswald Chambers*

—A PRAYER—

Dear Lord, keep me mindful that my riches are found in You. Deliver me from selfishness and greed. Let me share my possessions, both material and spiritual, with those in need. Let me be a humble, cheerful giver, Lord, and let the praise and glory be Yours.

—*Amen*

PRAISE

Make a joyful noise unto God, all ye lands: sing forth the honor of his name: make his praise glorious.

—Psalm 66:1-2 KJV

The heavens declare the glory of God; and the firmament showeth his handiwork.

—Psalm 19:1 KJV

Through Him then, let us continually offer up a sacrifice of praise to God, that is the fruit of lips that give thanks to His name.

—Hebrews 13:15 NASB

…in all your ways acknowledge him, and he will make your paths straight.

—Proverbs 3:6 NIV

Be still, and know that I am God….

—Psalm 46:10 KJV

*T*oday, as you hug your child or kiss your spouse, or as you gaze upon a passing cloud or marvel at a glorious sunset, think of what God has done for you and for yours. And, every time you notice a gift from the Giver of all things good, praise Him. His works are marvelous, His gifts are beyond understanding, and His love endures forever.

The Bible instructs—and experience teaches—that praising God results in our burdens' being lifted and our joys' being multiplied.

—Mary Prince

—A PRAYER—

*L*ord, Your gifts are greater than I can imagine, and Your love for me is greater than I can fathom. May I live each day with thanksgiving in my heart and praise on my lips. Thank You for the gift of Your Son and for the promise of eternal life. Let me share the joyous news of Jesus Christ with a world that needs His healing touch this day and every day.

—Amen

PRAYER

Watch ye therefore, and pray always....

—*Luke 21:36 KJV*

Rejoice evermore. Pray without ceasing. In every thing give thanks: for this is the will of God in Christ Jesus concerning you.

—*I Thessalonians 5:16-18 KJV*

...for your Father knows what you need, before you ask Him.

—*Matthew 6:8 NASB*

Ask and it shall be given to you; seek and you shall find; knock and it shall be opened to you. For every one who asks receives, and he who seeks finds, and to him who knocks it shall be opened.

—*Matthew 7:7 NASB*

Cast your burden upon the Lord and He will sustain you: He will never allow the righteous to be shaken.

—*Psalm 55:22 NASB*

*P*rayer changes things *and* it changes us. Today, instead of turning things over in your mind, turn them over to God in prayer. Instead of worrying about your next decision, ask God to lead the way. Don't limit your prayers to meals or to bedtime. Pray constantly about things great and small, and encourage your family to do so as well. God is listening, and He wants to hear from you.

Any concern too small to be turned into a prayer is too small to be made into a burden.

—*Corrie ten Boom*

—A Prayer—

*D*ear Lord, let me be a woman of prayer. Let me raise my hopes and my dreams, my worries and my fears to You. Let me be a worthy example to my children, showing them the importance and the power of prayer. Let me take everything to You in prayer, Dear Lord, and when I do, let me trust in Your answers.

—*Amen*

RENEWAL

Create in me a clean heart, O God; and renew a right spirit within me.

—*Psalm 51:10 KJV*

I will give you a new heart and put a new spirit in you....

—*Ezekiel 36: 26 NIV*

For He has satisfied the thirsty soul, and the hungry soul He has filled with what is good.

—*Psalm 107:9 NASB*

...let the hearts of those who seek the Lord rejoice. Look to the Lord and his strength; seek his face always.

—*I Chronicles 16:10-11 NIV*

Come to me all you who are weary and burdened, and I will give you rest. Take my yoke upon you and learn from me, for I am gentle and humble in heart, and you will find rest for your soul. For my yoke is easy and my burden is light.

—*Matthew 11:28-30 NIV*

*G*od intends that His children lead joyous lives filled with abundance and peace. But sometimes, as all mothers can attest, abundance and peace seem very far away. It is then that we must turn to God for renewal, and when we do, He will restore us. Are you tired or troubled? Turn your heart toward God in prayer. Are you weak or worried? Make the time to delve deeply into God's Holy Word. When you do, you'll discover that the Creator of the universe stands ready and able to create a new sense of wonderment and joy in you.

———

He is the God of wholeness and restoration.

—*Stormie Omartian*

—A Prayer—

*H*eavenly Father, sometimes I am troubled, and sometimes I grow weary. When I am weak, Lord, give me strength. When I am discouraged, Lord, renew me. When I am fearful, let me feel Your healing touch. Let me draw strength from Your promises and from Your unending love.

—*Amen*

RIGHTEOUSNESS

And let us not be weary in well doing: for in due season we shall reap, if we faint not.

—*Galatians 6:9 KJV*

And whatsoever ye do in word or deed, do all in the name of the Lord Jesus, giving thanks to God and the Father by him.

—*Colossians 3:17 KJV*

Thus you will walk in the ways of good men and keep the paths of the righteous. For the upright will live in the land, and the blameless will remain in it; but the wicked will be cut off from the land and the unfaithful will be torn from it.

—*Proverbs 2:20-22 NIV*

Jesus answered and said unto him, If a man love me, he will keep my words: and my Father will love him, and we will come unto him, and make our abode with him.

—*John 14:23 KJV*

Therefore as you have received Christ Jesus the Lord, so walk with him.

—*Colossians 2:6 NASB*

God has given us a guidebook for living righteously, the Holy Bible. It contains thorough instructions which, if followed, lead to fulfillment, righteousness and salvation. As Christians, we are called to study God's Word and to live by it. As parents, we must encourage our children to do the same.

———⟡———

Our progress in holiness depends on God and ourselves—on God's grace and on our will to be holy.

—*Mother Teresa*

—A PRAYER—

Lord, when I neglect the reading of Your Word, I suffer. But, when I turn my thoughts, my faith, my trust, and my prayers to You, I am blessed. Let me live righteously according to Your commandments, and let me discover Your will and follow Your Word this day and always.

—*Amen*

SALVATION

Everyone who calls on the name of the Lord will be saved.

—Romans 10:13 NIV

I tell you the truth, he who believes has everlasting life.

—John 6:47 NIV

For it is by grace you have been saved, through faith—and this not from yourselves, it is the gift of God....

—Ephesians 2:8 NIV

For God sent not his Son into the world to condemn the world; but that the world through him might be saved.

—John 3:17 KJV

These things have I written unto you that believe on the name of the Son of God; that ye may know that ye have eternal life....

—I John 5:13 KJV

The familiar words of *Ephesians 2:8* make God's promise perfectly clear: *For it is by grace you have been saved, through faith....* We are saved not because of our good deeds but because of our faith in Christ. May we, who have been given so much, praise our Savior throughout eternity.

———

Though the details may differ from story to story, we are all sinners—saved only by the wonderful grace of God.

—*Gloria Gaither*

—A PRAYER—

My salvation is in You, O Lord. My soul finds rest in You through Your Son Jesus Christ. The gift of salvation brings meaning to my life on earth and life eternal with You in heaven. Let me praise You and give thanks for Your glorious gift.

—*Amen*

SEEKING GOD

The LORD is with you when you are with him. If you seek him, he will be found by you....

—2 Chronicles 15:2 NIV

The LORD is good to those whose hope is in him, to the one who seeks Him....

—Lamentations 3:25 NIV

This is what the LORD says to the house of Israel: "Seek me and live...."

—Amos 5:4 NIV

But if from there you seek the LORD your God, you will find him if you look for him with all your heart and with all your soul.

—Deuteronomy 4:29 NIV

But seek first his kingdom and his righteousness, and all these things will be given to you as well.

—Matthew 6:33 NIV

Where is God? He is everywhere you have ever been and everywhere you will ever go. He is with you night and day; He knows your every thought; He hears every heartbeat. When you earnestly seek Him, you will find Him because He is here, waiting patiently for you to reach out to Him…right here.

———

We rarely discover anything monumental about God without discovering something momentous about ourselves. With every revelation comes an invitation to adjust out lives to what we have seen.

—*Beth Moore*

—A PRAYER—

How comforting it is, Lord, to know that if I seek You, I will find You. Let me reach out to You, Heavenly Father, and let me praise You for revealing Your Word, Your way, and Your love.

—*Amen*

SERVING OTHERS

But a Samaritan, as he traveled, came where the man was; and when he saw him, he took pity on him. He went to him and bandaged his wounds, pouring on oil and wine. Then he put the man on his own donkey, took him to an inn and took care of him.

—*Luke 10:33,34 NIV*

Suppose a brother or a sister is without clothes and daily food. If one of you says to him, "Go, I wish you well; keep warm and well fed," but does nothing about his physical needs, what good is it?

—*James 2:15,16 NIV*

...but whosoever will be great among you, let him be your minister; and whosoever will be chief among you, let him be your servant: even as the Son of man came not to be ministered unto, but to minister, and to give his life a ransom for many.

—*Matthew 20:26-28 KJV*

Therefore all things whatsoever ye would that men should do to you, do ye even so to them: for this is the law and the prophets.

—*Matthew 7:12 KJV*

When Jesus was tempted by Satan, the Master's response was unambiguous. Jesus chose to worship the Lord *and serve him only*. We, as followers of Christ, must follow in His footsteps. When we place God in a position of secondary importance, we do ourselves great harm. But, when we imitate Jesus and place the Lord in His rightful place—at the center of our lives—then we claim spiritual treasures that will endure forever.

———◆———

In God's family, there is to be one great body of people: servants. In fact, that's the way to the top in his kingdom.

—Chuck Swindoll

—A Prayer—

Dear Lord, sometimes I am distracted by the busyness and confusion of daily life. But, if I stray from You, Lord, I suffer. Let me serve You first, Lord, and let me place my devotion to You above every other aspect of my life, today and forever.

—Amen

SHARING

You are the light of the world. A city on a hill cannot be hidden. Neither do people light a lamp and put it in under a bowl. Instead they put it on its stand, and it gives light to everyone in the house. In the same way, let your light shine before men, that they may see your good deeds and praise your Father in heaven.

—*Matthew 5:14-16 NIV*

In everything I did, I showed you that by this kind of hard work we must help the weak, remembering the words the Lord Jesus himself said: "It is more blessed to give than to receive."

—*Acts 20:35 NIV*

He that hath two coats, let him impart to him that hath none; and he that hath meat, let him do likewise.

—*Luke 3:11 KJV*

…the righteous give without sparing.

—*Proverbs 21:26 NIV*

We live in a fast-paced, competitive world where it is easy to say, "Me first." But, God instructs us to do otherwise. In God's kingdom, those who proclaim, "Me first," are last. God loves a cheerful, selfless giver. If we seek greatness in God's eyes, we must look our neighbors squarely in the eye and say, "You first." When you do, we will lead our families in the footsteps of the humble servant who died for our sins: Christ Jesus.

———

To show great love for God and our neighbor, we need not do great things. It is how much love we put in the doing that makes our offering something beautiful for God.

—Mother Teresa

—A Prayer—

Lord, I know there is no happiness in keeping Your blessings to myself. True joy is found in sharing what I have with others. Make me a generous, loving, humble servant, Dear Lord, as I follow the example of Your Son Jesus.

—Amen

STRENGTH

But the Lord is my defence; and my God is the rock of my refuge.

—Psalm 94:22 KJV

Cast thy burden upon the Lord, and he shall sustain thee; he shall never suffer the righteous to be moved.

—Psalm 55:22 KJV

...I do not consider myself yet to have taken hold of it. But one thing I do: Forgetting what is behind and straining toward what is ahead, I press on toward the goal to win the prize for which God has called me heavenward in Christ Jesus.

—Philippians 3:13,14 NIV

For I the LORD thy God will hold thy right hand, saying unto thee, Fear not; I will help thee.

—Isaiah 41:13 KJV

God is our refuge and strength, a very present help in trouble.

—Psalm 46:1 KJV

God is a never-ending source of strength and courage for those who call upon Him. In difficult times, God is there. When we see no hope, God reminds us of His promises. When we grieve, God wipes away our tears. Whatever our circumstances, God will protect us and care for us...if we let Him.

———◆———

He stands fast as your rock, steadfast as your safeguard, sleepless as your watcher, valiant as your champion.

—C. H. Spurgeon

—A Prayer—

Lord, sometimes life is difficult. Sometimes, I am worried, weary, or heartbroken. But, when I lift my eyes to You, Lord, You strengthen me. When I am weak, You lift me up. Today, let me turn to You, Lord, for my strength and my salvation.

—Amen

Testimony

Also I say unto you, Whosoever shall confess me before men, him shall the Son of man also confess before the angels of God: but he that denieth me before men shall be denied before the angels of God.

—Luke 12:8-9 KJV

...in your hearts set apart Christ as Lord. Always be prepared to give an answer to everyone who asks you to give the reason for the hope that you have.

—I Peter 3:15 NIV

And the night following, the Lord stood by him, and said, be of good cheer, Paul: for...thou hast testified of me....

—Acts 23:11 KJV

And whosoever shall not receive you, nor hear you, when ye depart thence, shake off the dust under your feet for a testimony against them.

—Mark 6:12 KJV

In his second letter to Timothy, Paul shares a message to believers of every generation when he writes, "God has not given us a spirit of timidity." Paul's meaning is clear: When sharing our testimonies, we, as Christians, must be courageous, forthright, and unashamed. As parents, our first obligation is to share our faith with our children, but we must not stop there. We must also share our testimonies with a world that desperately needs to hear the healing message of God's grace.

———————

God has ordained that others may see the reality of His presence by the illumination our lives shed forth.

—Beth Moore

—A Prayer—

Dear Lord, the life that I live and the words that I speak bear testimony to my faith. Make me a faithful servant of Your Son Jesus. Let me be a godly example to my children, and let my testimony be worthy of You. Let my words be sure and true, Lord, and let my actions point others to You.

—Amen

THANKSGIVING

Make a joyful noise unto the Lord all ye lands. Serve the lord with gladness: come before his presence with singing. Know ye that the Lord he is God: it is he that hath made us, and not we ourselves; we are his people and the sheep of his pasture. Enter into his gates with thanksgiving, and into his courts with praise; be thankful unto him and bless his name. For the Lord is good; his mercy is everlasting; and his truth endureth to all generations.

—*Psalm 100:1-5 KJV*

It is good to give thanks to the Lord, to sing praises to the Most High. It is good to proclaim your unfailing love in the morning, your faithfulness in the evening.

—*Psalm 92:2-3 NLT*

And let the peace of God rule in your hearts...and be ye thankful.

—*Colossians 3:15 KJV*

As believing Christians, we are blessed beyond measure. Thanksgiving should become a habit, a regular part of our daily routines. God has blessed us beyond measure, and we owe Him everything, including our eternal praise. To paraphrase the familiar children's blessing, "God is great, God is good, let us thank Him for…everything!"

———

The ability to rejoice in any situation is a sign of spiritual maturity.

—Billy Graham

—A Prayer—

Thank You, Lord, for the gift of eternal life and for the gift of eternal love. Let me share the Good News of Your Son Jesus with thanksgiving forever in my heart and praise forever upon my lips.

—Amen

TODAY

This is the day which the Lord hath made; we will rejoice and be glad in it.

—*Psalm 118:24 KJV*

...I know whom I have believed, and am convinced that he is able to guard what I have entrusted to him for that day.

—*II Timothy 1:12 NIV*

O come, let us sing unto the LORD: let us make a joyful noise to the rock of our salvation. Let us come before his presence with thanksgiving, and make a joyful noise unto him with psalms.

—*Psalm 95:1-2 KJV*

The heavens declare the glory of God; and the firmament showeth his handiwork.

—*Psalm 19:1 KJV*

The LORD is my strength and song, and He has become my salvation; He is my God, and I will praise Him....

—*Exodus 15:2 NKJV*

For Christian believers, every day begins and ends with God and His Son. Christ came to this earth to give us abundant life and eternal salvation. We give thanks to our Maker when we treasure each day and use it to the fullest. Today, may we give thanks for this day and for the One who created it.

Submit each day to God, knowing that He is God over all your tomorrows.

—*Kay Arthur*

—A Prayer—

Help me, Father, to learn from the past but not live in it. And, help me to plan for the future but not to worry about it. This is the day You have given me, Lord. Let me use it according to Your master plan, and let me give thanks for Your blessings. Enable me to live each moment to the fullest, totally involved in Your will.

—*Amen*

TRUST IN GOD

Do not let your hearts be troubled. Trust in God; trust also in me. In my Father's house are many rooms; if it were not so, I would have told you. I am going there to prepare a place for you.

—John 14:1,2 NIV

We...worship by the Spirit of God...glory in Christ Jesus, and...put no confidence in the flesh....

—Philippians 3:3 NIV

It is better to trust in the LORD than to put confidence in man. It is better to trust in the LORD than to put confidence in princes.

—Psalm 118:8-9 KJV

The LORD is my rock, and my fortress, and my deliverer; my God, my strength, in whom I will trust....

—Psalm 18:2 KJV

...the Lord's unfailing love surrounds the man who trusts in him.

—Psalm 32:10 NIV

Do you seek God's blessings for yourself and your family? Then trust Him. Trust Him with every aspect of your life. Trust Him with your relationships. Trust Him with your finances. Follow His commandments and pray for His guidance. Then, wait patiently for God's revelations and for His blessings. In His own fashion and in His own time, God will bless you in ways that you never could have imagined.

Trust the past to God's mercy, the present to God's love and the future to God's providence.

—*St. Augustine*

—A Prayer—

Lord, when I trust in things of this earth, I will be disappointed. But, when I put my faith in You, I am secure. You are my rock and my shield. When I am worried, Lord, let me trust in You. You will love me and protect me, and You will share Your boundless grace today, tomorrow, and forever.

—*Amen*

TRUTH

These are the things you are to do: Speak the truth to each other, and render true and sound judgment in your courts....

—*Zechariah 8:16 NIV*

...as we have received mercy, we faint not; but have renounced the hidden things of dishonesty, not walking in craftiness, nor handling the word of God deceitfully; but, by manifestation of the truth, commending ourselves to every man's conscience in the sight of God.

—*II Corinthians 4:1-2 KJV*

To this end was I born, and for this cause came I into the world, that I should bear witness unto the truth.

—*John 18:37 KJV*

Jesus answered, "I am the way and the truth and the life. No one comes to the Father except through me."

—*John 14:6 NIV*

The words of *John 8:32* are both familiar and profound: *ye shall know the truth, and the truth shall make you free.* Truth is God's way: He commands His children to live in truth, and He rewards those who follow his commandment. Jesus is the personification of a perfect, liberating truth that offers salvation to mankind. Do you seek to walk with God? Then take your children's hands and walk in truth as you walk with the Savior.

———

Those who walk in truth walk in liberty.

—*Beth Moore*

—A Prayer—

Dear Lord, You command Your children to walk in truth. Let me follow Your commandment. Give me the courage to speak honestly, and let me walk righteously with You so that others might see Your eternal truth reflected in my words and my deeds.

—*Amen*

WISDOM

The fear of the Lord is the beginning of wisdom: a good understanding have all they that do his commandments: his praise endureth for ever.

—*Psalm 111:10 KJV*

So teach us to number our days, that we may present to You a heart of wisdom.

—*Psalm 90:12 NASB*

For the Lord gives wisdom, and from his mouth come knowledge and understanding.

—*Proverbs 2:6 NIV*

But if any of you lacks wisdom, let him ask of God, who gives to all generously and without reproach, and it will be given to him.

—*James 1:5 NASB*

Wisdom is a tree of life to those who eat her fruit; happy is the man who keeps on eating it.

—*Proverbs 3:18 TLB*

Wisdom is like a savings account: If you add to it consistently, then eventually you will have accumulated a great sum. The secret to success is consistency. Do you seek wisdom for yourself and for your family? Then keep learning and keep motivating them to do likewise. The ultimate source of wisdom, of course, is the Word of God. When you read God's Word and live according to His commandments, you will become wise.

If you lack knowledge, go to school. If you lack wisdom, get on your knees.

—Vance Havner

—A PRAYER—

I seek wisdom, Lord, not as the world gives, but as You give. Lead me in Your ways and teach me from Your Word so that, in time, my wisdom might glorify Your kingdom, Lord, and Your Son.

—Amen

>>
WORK
>>

But this I say, He which soweth sparingly shall reap also sparingly; and he which soweth bountifully shall reap also bountifully.

—II Corinthians 9:6 KJV

The plans of the diligent lead to profit as surely as haste leads to poverty.

—Proverbs 21:5 NIV

Whatever your hand finds to do, do it with all your might....

—Ecclesiastes 9:10 NIV

Whatever you do, work at it with all your heart, as working for the Lord, not for men.

—Colossians 3:23 NIV

But as for you, be strong and do not give up, for your work will be rewarded.

—II Chronicles 15:7 NIV

Motherhood is not only the most rewarding profession, it is also the most demanding. Mothers seldom, if ever, get a day off. And when the sun goes down, there is no rest for Mom until her head hits the pillow. And does all this hard work pay off? Of course it does...every time she hears those familiar words, "I love you Mom!"

⟐

Ordinary work, which is what most of us do most of the time, is ordained by God every bit as much as is the extraordinary.

—*Elisabeth Elliot*

—A Prayer—

Heavenly Father, You know that motherhood is difficult work. When I am tired, give me strength. When I become frustrated, give me patience. When I lose sight of Your purpose for my life, give me a passion for my daily responsibilities. Let me raise my children to be Your loving, faithful servants, and let all the honor and glory be Yours.

—*Amen*

WORRY

Therefore do not worry about tomorrow, for tomorrow will worry about itself. Each day has enough trouble of its own.

—*Matthew 6:34 NIV*

Yea, though I walk through the valley of the shadow of death, I will fear no evil: for thou art with me; thy rod and thy staff they comfort me.

—*Psalm 23:4 KJV*

Cast your burden upon the Lord and He will sustain you: He will never allow the righteous to be shaken.

—*Psalm 55:22 NASB*

Trust in him at all times, O people; pour out your hearts to him, for God is our refuge.

—*Psalm 62:8 NIV*

Daughter, be of good comfort; thy faith hath made thee whole.

—*Matthew 9:24 KJV*

If you are a mother, it is simply a fact of life: You worry. You worry about health, about finances, about safety, about education, and about countless other challenges of life, some great and some small. Where is the best place to take your worries? Take them to God. Take your troubles to Him, and your fears, and your sorrows. Seek protection from the One who cannot be moved.

———◆———

Worry is a cycle of inefficient thoughts whirling around a center of fear.

—*Corrie ten Boom*

—A Prayer—

Lord, when my faith begins to wane, Help me to trust You more. Then, with Your Holy Word on my lips and with the love of Your Son in my heart, let me live courageously, faithfully, prayerfully, and thankfully today and every day.

—*Amen*

WORSHIP

Happy are those who hear the joyful call to worship, for they will walk in the light of your presence, Lord.

—Psalm 89:15 NLT

I was glad when they said unto me, Let us go into the house of the LORD.

—Psalm 122:1 KJV

Enter into his gates with thanksgiving, *and* into his courts with praise: be thankful unto him, *and* bless his name.

—Psalm 100:4 KJV

Then saith Jesus unto him, Get thee hence, Satan: for it is written, Thou shalt worship the Lord thy God, and him only shalt thou serve.

—Matthew 4:10 KJV

But seek first his kingdom and his righteousness, and all these things will be given to you as well.

—Matthew 6:33 NIV

When we worship God, either alone or in the company of fellow believers, we are blessed. When we fail to worship God, for whatever reason, we forfeit the spiritual riches that are rightfully ours. Every day provides opportunities to put God where He belongs: at the center of our lives. Let us worship Him, and only Him, today and always.

In the sanctuary, we discover beauty: the beauty of His presence.

—*Kay Arthur*

—A PRAYER—

When I worship You, Lord, You direct my path and You cleanse my heart. Let today and every day be a time of worship and praise. And, let me worship You in everything that I think and do.

—*Amen*